TOOTS™
GIFT BOOKS
You *Can* Judge a Book by its Cover!

Exclusively Distributed in North Americc by

pavilion gift
COMPANY®

www.tootsgiftbooks.com

THE WORLD OF
CIGARS

Michelle Brachet

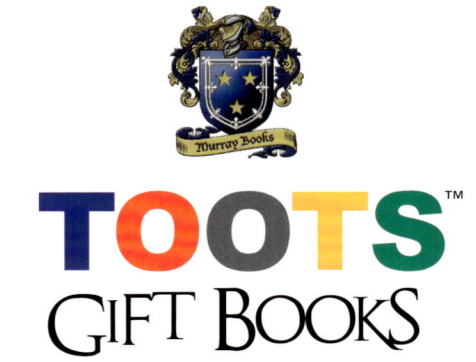

TOOTS™
GIFT BOOKS
You *Can* Judge a Book by its Cover!

www.tootsbooks.com

First published in 2011
This edition published in 2013
by Murray Books (Australia)
www.murraybooks.com

ISBN 978-0-9871735-0-8

Design and Production: Peter Murray

Author Michelle Brachet

Exclusively Distributed in North America by

pavilion gift
COMPANY

www.tootsgiftbooks.com

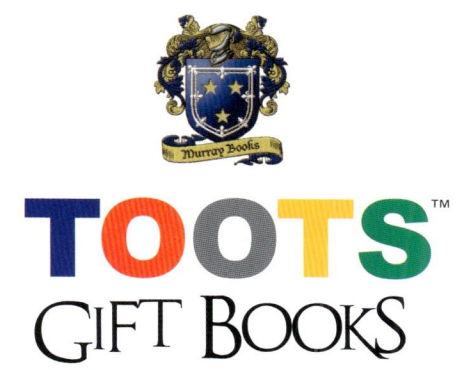

TOOTS™
GIFT BOOKS
You *Can* Judge a Book by its Cover!

Contents

Introduction

◆

Cigars are made from dried and fermented tobacco leaves tightly rolled so that they can be lit, will burn evenly and can be smoked. Cigars come in thousands of different sizes, colours and brands, and the variety in taste and character is therefore quite endless. They can be mass-produced by machine, but the finest cigars in the world are made from the best quality tobacco possible and rolled individually by hand. These premium cigars can fetch a high price and are what true cigar-smoking connoisseurs collect and enjoy the most.

The word cigar originates from the Mayan-Indian word for smoking, 'sikar' and 'sicar', which means to smoke rolled tobacco leaves. This became 'cigarro' in Spanish. It was not until around 1730, however, that the actual word and its variants were used to describe what we now call cigars.

Premium cigars and cigar smoking has for a long time in the Western world been associated with power, leadership and to a certain extent wealth. Kings, politicians, presidents, famous generals and gentlemen in history have all smoked cigars. Quite unlike the cigarette in more ways than just constitution, cigars and social trends and traditions have gone hand in hand for hundreds of years. The fine cigar symbolises elegance, refinement and luxury.

Tobacco is grown all over the world, although like most commercial agricultural crops the best tobacco that makes the world's finest cigars come from specific regions such as Cuba, where the climate and soil conditions are ideal for growing the very best crops possible.

History of Cigars

◆

Tobacco is the product of an agricultural process made from the leaves of the genus Nicotiana plant. Historically it has been used for many other purposes as well as smoking including medicinal, chewing, snuffing, and particularly in the Americas has long been in use as an entheogen; tobacco could be found spread widely over all the islands of the Caribbean.

All Native American tribes had long used tobacco before the Western world discovered it, and the belief was that it was a gift from God and that by smoking it the smoke exhaled would carry thoughts and prayers to heaven.

When Christopher Columbus dropped anchor in October 1492 just off the Cuban coast, it is reported that the two men sent ashore described seeing natives with 'smoking heads'; smoking and the tobacco plant had been discovered. The tobacco seeds were brought back to Europe and quickly other European sailors also discovered the plant. Soon smoking tobacco had reached Spain and Portugal. France is thought to have followed when Jean Nicot, the French ambassador to Portugal, sent it in 1559 to the court of Catherine de Medici for medicinal purposes; the words nicotiana and nicotine were named in his honour. This new habit then spread to Italy, and Britain following Sir Walter Raleigh's voyages to the Americas. Within eighty years of Columbus's first encounter with it, the new plant from the New World had become a widely used commodity throughout the Old World. By the first decade of the seventeenth century tobacco was being grown commercially for the first time in North America.

Whilst cigarette smoking was still comparatively rare, cigar smoking was very common during the nineteenth century and was intrinsically linked to the class system and social etiquette of the Victorian period; gentlemen only would retire to the 'smoking room' after dinner to smoke cigars and discuss matters of a 'serious' nature away from

History of Cigars

the ladies. The cigar industry was also important to the economies of countries as many people were employed to make the cigars prior to the Industrial Revolution and the onset of machine manufacturing.

By the early twentieth century the United States was home to around eighty thousand cigar-making businesses, most of which constituted small family-run operations. These cigars would be rolled by hand in the shop and sold straight away.

Historically, cigar smoking has always had its opponents. Queen Victoria totally disapproved of tobacco smoking and it was not allowed anywhere in her vicinity. It was therefore a great relief to all gentlemen and nobility the day her son Edward VII came to the throne in 1901 and announced from Buckingham Palace, 'Gentlemen, you may proceed to smoke'. Smoking was also fought against in the United States, and those who fought the likes of 'demon rum' and brought about Prohibition in 1919 were also responsible for the fight against tobacco.

Despite these inconvenient attempts at obstruction, by the turn of the twentieth century a lot of pictures taken or images drawn of gentlemen, politicians, aristocrats and the like from all over the Western world have two things in common; many are wearing a hat, and many are holding a cigar.

In 1907 Alfred Dunhill opened a shop dedicated to fine tobacco products as the tradition of premium, hand-rolled Havana cigars continued particularly throughout Europe. Two of his most prestigious regular clients included Winston Churchill and Rudyard Kipling. As well as being an outstanding marketer for his business, Dunhill was also one of the first premium cigar business owners to realise the importance of humidifying and aging his cigars before selling them. He went on to open his New York shop in 1921.

The onset of World War I had a particularly beneficial impact on the tobacco industry as a whole. Cigarettes were, prior to the war, seen as rather effeminate compared with cigars. Due to the fact that they could be mass-produced

and packed with rations, however, the cigarette manufacturers got a big boost from an otherwise totally destructive war. In response to this the cigar producers had to move quickly in order to maintain their percentage of market share and they quickly developed machine-made cigars. Cigar prices therefore naturally plummeted and in the United States particularly, by the time the Great Depression had set in the machine-made cigar had become affordable even for the working classes.

World War II had a further impact on the cigar industry, which was a catalyst for the diffusion of cigar production throughout the Caribbean. The war meant that the premium Havana cigars were no longer available and British smokers in particular relied on premium cigars from Jamaica instead.

Cigar retailer Zino Davidoff also saw his career and business flourish over the war years similar to Alfred Dunhill's, and they are both regarded as twentieth-century cigar retailer figureheads. Davidoff and his family opened their first tobacco shop in 1929 in Geneva. During the early 1940's he managed to buy a large quantity of Havana cigars that the Vichy French government had owned. He therefore had a monopoly on the European market, as Havana cigars could not be bought anywhere else.

Hand-rolled Cuban cigars became extremely popular in the United States following World War II and smokers rejected their own mass-produced cigars in favour of the true Havana or 'clear Havana' (cigars made in the U.S. from imported Cuban tobacco). This, however, came to an abrupt end in 1962 when relations between President John F. Kennedy and Fidel Castro deteriorated and President Kennedy imposed a total trade embargo on Cuba; this is still in place today.

During the last thirty years or so of the twentieth century two important developments occurred, both of which had a marked impact on the cigar industry as a whole. The first reports from medical research proving that smoking tobacco was a contributing factor to getting cancer were released during the 1960's. At first, however, there was a dis-

History of Cigars

tinction between cigarette smoking, which is inhaled, and cigar smoking, which is not supposed to be inhaled and therefore a lesser risk to health. Initially, perhaps because of this distinction, cigar smoking remained popular for the following decade. Cigar smoking only started to decline as anti-smoking campaigns and legislation gathered momentum all over the world, which were based on further and more conclusive research.

The effect of the United States trade embargo on Cuba was also a catalyst for change. Some Cuban cigar makers moved to other countries and continued their businesses under the same brand name as before. This is where some confusion can occur due to the fact that the business they had left behind were taken over by Fidel Castro loyalists who also kept trading under the same brand names. It is therefore possible to buy two cigars with exactly the same name but from different countries of origin. The only way to know, for example, if a Montecristo, Cohiba, Romeo y Julieta, Fonseca or H. Upmann, to name a few, is from Cuba is if there is a small Habano or Havana stamped on the cigar band.

The gap in the United States cigar market left by the Cuban embargo also opened the door for many cigar-makers from other countries to expand their businesses significantly and many new premium cigars became available from other countries.

The world's peak in cigar smoking and demand will perhaps never equal that of the 1970's. Those who continue to enjoy fine cigars, however, may be smoking fewer than before but they are still as finely made as ever and the choice available is quite phenomenal. There are hundreds of cigar brands, and quality and prestigious cigars are still handmade and can be identified by the stamp of 'totalmente a mano' (totally by hand) or 'hecho a mano' (made by hand) on the box.

What Makes a Cigar

Three types of tobacco leaf make up the composition of cigars and are known as wrappers, fillers and binders. The different variation of each of these components determines a cigar's overall flavour and smoking characteristics.

The wrapper is the leaf used for the outermost part of a cigar and the leaves used are the widest from the plant. The wrapper constitutes about forty percent of a cigar's overall flavour and they can vary dramatically in taste and colour; over one hundred have been identified. In fact the whole cigar can be described based on the colour of its wrapper. The variations in colour of a wrapper leaf is the result of the processing method used as well as the fact that different varieties of tobacco have natural differences in colour. The amount of sun exposure the leaf has been subjected to is also a contributing factor.

Although there are many different shades of wrapper there are several most common classifications and even though there are subtle variations within these, from light to dark they are known as follows:

Double Claro – once popular but now rare, this variety is very light and slightly green, achieved by picking the leaves prior to full maturity and drying quickly. It is also known as Candela, American Market Selection or jade.

Claro – is a light tan colour, sometimes yellowish. This variety of wrapper indicates that the tobacco plant was shade-grown.

Colorado Claro – is medium brown in colour. The description English Market Selection is also typical of this variety but not solely; it can also refer to other wrappers in between the strengths of Double Claro and Maduro (see below).

What Makes a Cigar

Colorado – this wrapper has a distinctive reddish-brown colour and is also known as Rosado or Corojo.

Colorado Maduro – is darker brown in colour and is often associated with the Cuban-seed wrapper from Honduras and Nicaragua as well as the African Cameroon wrapper.

Maduro – predominantly grown in Nicaragua, Brazil, Mexico and Connecticut in the United States, this wrapper is very dark brown or black. The description of Spanish Market Selection can also encompass this variety.

Oscuro – mostly grown in Cuba, Nicaragua, Mexico, Brazil and Connecticut, this wrapper is black and sometimes appears oily. It is also known as Double Maduro and also applies to the description of Spanish Market Selection.

The filler is found inside the wrapper leaf, constitutes most of the cigar and consists of wrapped up bunches of leaves. Depending on which part of the plant the filler leaves come from very much influences the flavour, strength and overall quality of the final cigar. Cigars are usually made from a blend of various strengths of filler leaves and can be either long or short. A long filler uses whole leaves and produces the better quality cigars. Short fillers or 'mixed' are made up of chopped leaves and stems.

The filler or blend of filler used also has an effect on how the cigar burns. The short fillers burn hotter and can often leave pieces of leaf in a smoker's mouth. Long-filled cigars of excellent quality should burn both consistently and evenly.

Finally binders are leaves that have been rejected because of substandard quality (blemishes, discolouration, excess veins for example) and are used to hold the bunches of fillers together within the wrapper instead.

Tobacco Growing Regions

Tobacco is what is known as genetically stable. This means that the seeds of the plant remains genetically the same generation after generation. The reason that cigars made from tobacco from different regions of the world do not taste identical, however, is because the tobacco plant is very much like the grape vine. The species planted may be identical all over the world, but the climate variations, soil conditions and growing methods used all have an influence on the resulting taste of the final product. Tobacco's ideal growing conditions are in regions where the climate is mild and humid, and the soil loamy.

Dark tobacco is used to make quality cigars and is predominantly grown in three tropical areas: Latin America and the Caribbean, near the South China Sea in East Asia, and West Africa.

Cuba

Perhaps poignant is the fact that Cuban tobacco was in fact the first to be exported. To this day many cigar smokers still consider Cuban tobacco and their premium hand-rolled cigars to be the very best in the world.

This is due to the fact that Cuba has arguably the best tobacco-growing plantations in the world. In the westernmost province of Cuba is the Vuelta Abajo, which makes up most of Pinar del Rìo. The rich red soil in this region is planted with approximately one hundred thousand acres of cigar tobacco. Particularly well known for its wrapper leaves is the town of San Luis, where Alejandro Robaina, Cuba's most famous tobacco farmer lives. San Juan y Martinez is

also a small town that produces some of the best tobacco in the world.

Cuba has about fifty government-run cigar factories on the island. Most plantations of around one hundred and fifty acres are privately owned or part of small cooperatives. The growers sell the tobacco to the Ministry of Agriculture for fixed prices, and before sending it to the government cigar factories, they process and age the crop. The very best factories can be found in and around Havana. Each factory produces a mix of simple unbranded cigars for domestic sale as well as a number of different brands for the export market.

The region of Partido is arguably second only to Vuelta Abajo and is situated just southwest of Havana. This area specialises in wrapper tobacco for quality cigars due for export. A certain amount of Connecticut-seed wrappers are also produced here that are then sold to cigar manufacturers in Europe.

Other tobacco-growing areas of Cuba include the Semi-Vuelta (also in Pinar del Rìo), Remedios and Oriente in the southeast.

Dominican Republic

Tobacco growing in the Dominican Republic became significant following the Cuban trade embargo by the United States. As the Havana cigar market disappeared overnight, cigar-manufacturing businesses had to look elsewhere to find land suitable for growing tobacco of the same quality; and they found it in Cuba's neighbour. The Dominican Republic now produces the world's largest amount of premium handmade cigars.

Regarded as the very best tobacco-growing region is the Yaque Valley. It is six miles wide and runs about twenty-

Tobacco Growing Regions

———————————◆———————————

five miles from Santiago city to the town of Esperanza. Although more and more cigar-makers are beginning to grow their own tobacco, traditionally the majority of tobacco farmers would sell their produce to packers called 'empacadores'. The empacadores are responsible for processing the tobacco and then selling to the manufacturers.

Honduras and Nicaragua

Sharing a border in Central America, both Honduras and Nicaragua have, for different reasons, had serious problems over the past few decades but are both now recovering quickly and are really beginning to flourish.

The tobacco from Honduras is predominantly grown from the Cuban-seed variety, which is one of their most important unique selling points due to the fact that they can claim their cigars taste more like true Havana cigars than any others.

Unfortunately the only problem with Cuban-seed tobacco is that it is particularly susceptible to disease. In the mid-1980's the Honduras tobacco plantations were hit by a plague of blue mould. The result of this meant that cigars produced in the country were then made with tobacco of a lesser quality, which damaged the region's hitherto world-renowned reputation. Ways of fighting blue mould have since been found and Honduras's reputation for producing quality and rich tasting cigars is back on track.

Again during the 1980's, Nicaragua's cigar industry endured serious setbacks due to the country's ten-year-long civil war between Sandinista government forces and the United States-backed Contras. The heaviest fighting occurred over the tobacco-growing areas and the crops were devastated.

Tobacco Growing Regions

Nicaragua's comeback from this has, however, been fairly remarkable and by 1996 it had recovered sufficiently to become the third largest cigar exporter to the United States, jumping ahead of Jamaica and Mexico and only behind the Dominican Republic and Honduras. Its cigar exports continue to grow at an impressive rate.

Mexico

Mexico has two tobacco-growing regions both of which are in the state of Veracruz on the south of the Gulf Coast. The northern part of the state specialises in producing filler tobacco and a black native 'tobacco negro', which is used for maduro wrappers. The southern regions' speciality is a strain of the Sumatra-seed tobacco, which is revered for its leaves' delicate and silky structure. This is used for wrappers and binders. Maduro wrappers are also grown in the south but specifically in the San Andres Valley.

Ecuador

The South American country of Ecuador grows Connecticut-seed and Sumatra-seed plant varieties and is especially regarded for producing high-quality wrapper leaves. The country's tobacco-growing regions are mostly covered in cloud giving the plants prolonged natural shade. The result of this produces leaves of excellent colour with a light vein structure, which are silky to the touch.

Tobacco Growing Regions

Brazil

The majority of cigar tobacco grown in Brazil comes from a native variety called Mata Fina. The main region of production is situated on the central east coast in Bahia. The native Mata Fina produces tobacco leaves that are slightly sweet yet dark and richly flavoured, and are often used for premium cigar filler.

Just north of Bahia lies Alagoas and is the home to another native plant variety called Arapiraca, although due to the fact that the leaves lack flavour in comparison with many others, it is not grown and used so much today.

Connecticut

Connecticut is in the state of New England and is the only tobacco-growing region that breaks the tropical climate rule. North of Hartford lies the Connecticut River Valley, which produces one of the cigar industry's finest wrappers called Connecticut Shade. This leaf is mild to medium in taste, is fine to the touch but has an element of elasticity about it, and has a golden tan appearance.

A more dark, sun-grown tobacco is also grown in Connecticut. Called Connecticut Broadleaf, it is has more distinct veins, is thicker than the Connecticut Shade and is used mostly for dark maduro wrappers.

Tobacco Growing Regions

Cameroon and Central African Republic

Both of these West African nations grow a very high-quality Sumatra-seed tobacco leaf called Cameroon wrapper. Its colour varies from greenish-brown to dark brown and it is renowned for its, albeit neutral, but very pleasant flavours. The Cameroon wrapper also has a unique texture or grain that is described as 'tooth'. The structure and flavour combinations of this leaf make it ideal for use as a wrapper for full-flavoured cigars.

Indonesia and The Philippines

The Sumatra-seed leaf (also known as Java seed) is grown in various places all over the world, but its source of origin is the archipelago of Indonesia. The pure and original form of the Sumatra-seed leaf is neutral in flavour, mostly dark brown in colour and is used mainly as wrapper tobacco for small cigars.

Next door and north-east of Indonesia, the Philippines also produce cigar tobacco. It is produced from a hybrid strain of tobacco plant and although mild in flavour it is pleasantly aromatic.

Handmade Cigars

◆

Making consistently good quality handmade cigars is an art, and a complex one at that. This time-honoured tradition requires the perfect combination of experienced tobacco farmers, master blenders, and skilled cigar-rollers. If all these elements are in place premium cigars can be boxed, exported, sold and smoked with immense pride.

Before the tobacco can be made into a cigar, it first has to be cured. After harvesting it is usually stored in a barn for between thirty and forty days in order for this to happen. Next is the fermentation stage, which initiates a 'sweating' of the tobacco. The tobacco is moistened a little and then stacked in piles or large bales. The temperature inside the bales can reach as high as sixty degrees Celsius, which causes the tobacco to 'sweat'. In some cases the bales can be turned over and remoistened three or four times before the fermentation process is finished. The reason for fermenting the tobacco in such as way is to allow ammonia to be released, which reduces the total content of nicotine.

Once the fermentation process is complete, the bales of tobacco (usually covered in Hessian cloth) are then allowed to age. Although lighter tobacco can be ready in about a year, some manufacturers can age their tobacco for ten years or more. Once ready to be handed over to the blender and cigar-rollers, the tobacco is made more supple by being dampened slightly.

To create a premium cigar with the correct balance in taste, strength and consistency of burn requires the skill and creativity of a master blender. The number of different tobaccos used depends on the required thickness or 'ring

Handmade Cigars

---

gauge' of the final cigar and can be a blend of between two and four different varieties. The master blender then passes on the formula or recipe for a specific cigar to the roller.

The roller's job is to consistently make cigar after cigar exactly to the master blender's instructions. The roller places each different tobacco leaf to be used in separate boxes at the desk before beginning.

The roller then presses the filler leaves together in the hand before placing them on the binder leaf, which holds it all together. This is then rolled together to form a 'bunch', and the 'bunch' is then cut to the specified length and placed in a wooden mould. The wooden mould is put into a screw press for about an hour. The cigar is usually turned over and repressed half way through by the press operator.

Once pressed the roller can then apply the wrapper leaf to the bunch. Although the wrapper leaf can be one of numerous varieties and colours, they will all be supple and visually beautiful. Constant pressure has to be applied to the bunch as the wrapper is applied. It is then sealed at the head of the cigar with vegetable glue to prevent the cigar from unravelling.

Each individual hand-rolled cigar is then inspected by a supervisor. Any slight flaw or inconsistency, including significant weight variations, will result in the cigar being rejected or sent back to the rolling table. Normally weighed in bunches of fifty, a skilled and experienced cigar-roller can achieve less than one gram difference between five bunches of cigars.

The final stage for the cigars before they are checked for the last time, packed and shipped is a stay in the ageing room. The majority of cigars are aged for at least twenty-one days, but they can be aged for significantly longer periods than this, anywhere from ninety to one hundred and eighty days. The purpose of this process is to give the different tobaccos in the cigar a chance to marry and blend together, which ultimately creates a more balanced cigar when smoked.

A Cigar for Everyone

———————◆———————

Due to the enormous array of shapes and sizes that handmade cigars can come in, they are instead described by their length and width dimensions in addition to their shape; together this is known as the 'vitola'. In Cuba, the United Kingdom and the United States imperial measurements are used for the length, and the diameter is referred to in terms of ring gauge. The ring gauge is divided into sixty-fourths of an inch. For example, a cigar with a ring gauge of forty-two, has a diameter of forty-two, sixty-four fourths of an inch. In other countries metric measurements are used and the diameter of a cigar is described in millimetres. The world's finest cigars are only weighed in the factory for the sole purpose of quality control.

The actual size of a cigar has absolutely no bearing on its strength; a fact often misconstrued. A small cigar made with strong tobacco will be a strong smoke regardless of its size, the same as a very large cigar made from more mellow and mild tobacco will be just that.

In terms of cigar shapes, there are as many different ones as there are variations in colour shade and flavour. There are, however, two general categories that most cigars fall into: the Parejo and the Figurado.

A Parejo, or sometimes simply called a 'corona' is a straight-sided cigar and is the most common cigar shape. There are naturally many subtle differences between every one generally termed a parejo, but consistent characteristics include the closed 'head', which needs cutting before smoking, and the open 'foot', which is ready for lighting.

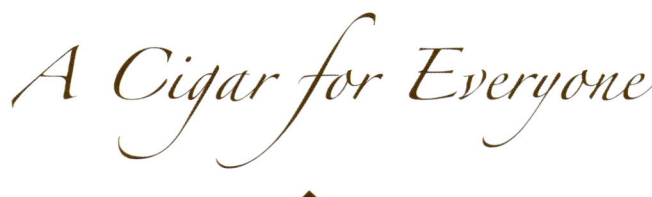

A Cigar for Everyone

Parejo cigars can then be broadly broken down into eight separate categories:

Petit Corona – a short corona, normally with a ring gauge of forty to forty-two and length of four and a half inches.

Corona – the ring gauge is normally between forty-two and forty-four, and the length is traditionally five and a half to six inches.

Churchill – this is a larger version of the corona with traditional dimensions of seven inches in length by a ring gauge of forty-eight.

Robusto – this is a shorter version of the Churchill and is becoming increasingly popular. Its traditional size is five to five and a half inches in length by an impressive ring gauge of fifty.

Corona Gorda – this is a long cigar of traditionally five and five-eighths inches with a ring gauge of forty-six.

Double Corona – has a standard length of seven and a half to eight inches and a ring gauge of forty-nine to fifty-two.

Panatela – this format varies more than others but in essence it is like a longer and thinner corona. Its length can vary from five to seven and a half inches and can have a ring gauge of anything from thirty-four to thirty-eight inches.

Lonsdale – generally this is longer than a corona but thicker than a panatela with a classic size of six and three-quarter inches in length with a ring gauge of forty-two to forty-four.

It is important to understand that the particular name for the type of cigar and resulting taste is not consistent from brand to brand; one company's panatela for example will taste completely different to another company's of the same category.

The term Figurado is used to describe an unusually shaped cigar, and there are a number of traditional cigar formats that encompass more novel shapes compared with the generic straight-sided cylinder shape that most cigars are. There are six different general terms for these, although not every cigar can be perfectly fitted into the constraints of

A Cigar for Everyone

$\diamond$

the following categories and some manufacturers descriptions may vary.

Pyramid – the name comes from the closed head that is sharply tapered in contrast to its wider open foot. These can be between six and seven inches long with a ring gauge of about forty at the head widening to fifty-two to fifty-four at the foot.

Belicoso – this shape was traditionally a shorter version of the pyramid of about five to five and a half inches long. The modern take on it means that it is now more like that of a corona or corona gorda with a tapered head.

Torpedo – this cigar has a pointed head, closed foot and a bulge in the middle.

Perfecto – this is similar to the torpedo in terms of closed foot and middle bulge. The head, however, is round rather than pointed. The overall dimensions of a perfecto can vary greatly. The length can range from four and a half to nine inches and ring gauge from thirty-eight to forty-eight.

Culebra – an extremely exotic-shaped cigar, it is made from three separate panatelas plaited and banded together to produce a single cigar. It is a good example of why cigars have been called 'ropes' in the past. The three parts are not smoked as one, however, but split from the band and enjoyed separately. They are normally five to six inches in length with a ring gauge of about thirty-eight. The culebra is unsurprisingly pretty rare in this day and age.

Diademas – this is a large cigar and has a closed and tapered head. The foot can be open or closed but it is at least eight inches long or longer with a ring gauge of fifty-two or greater.

Art and Etiquette

◆

Unlike smoking a cigarette, which is a matter of merely putting one in the mouth and lighting, cigars need a little more preparation before smoking. It is important to learn how to cut and light a cigar properly in order to get maximum quality and enjoyment out of it.

Almost all premium cigars have a closed head that must be cut before smoking and the better the cigar the more careful the cut required; a bad cut can ruin a cigar. There are various different ways to achieve this but the overall aim is create a smooth, big enough opening for smoking without damaging the structure of the cigar.

The safest way to cut the cigar is by using a sharp, purpose-made cigar cutter (double or single-bladed) that has a guillotine-like sharp blade to give a clean cut and smooth finish. Other methods include making a V-shaped wedge cut (also called a notch cut, cat's eye, wedge cut or English cut) which can expose a large area making it easy to draw on the cigar, but it can also mean that the cigar could burn too hot. Sharp knives can also be used but great skill and steady hands are required to do this properly. Biting the end off, as seen in the movies, is an option and some still do it, but has several drawbacks such as not being able to see, ending up with a mouthful of tobacco, and the risk of damaging the cigar, as teeth are not as sharp as proper cutters. There are also piercers and specifically designed cigar-cutting scissors.

Whichever cutting method is chosen, on most fine cigars, the cut should be made about two millimetres from the end, or at the point that the curved end of the cigar begins to straight out.

Art and Etiquette

———————————◆———————————

Once the cigar has been prepared at the head end, the foot of the cigar must then be lit properly. As with cutting, this has to be done properly otherwise the enjoyment of the cigar could be ruined. Lighting a cigar takes longer than lighting a cigarette and there are a few rules of thumb to ensure that it is lit correctly and therefore burns evenly, which is the key. The first rule is never to use a lighter or matches that may influence the taste of the tobacco. Butane lighters are ideal as it is an odourless, clean burn, whereas matches and fluid-filled lighters can impart undesirable tastes to the cigar. Using wooden matches that haven't been treated and soaked in sulphur is a good alternative, but a proper cigar lighter is ideal as it uses odourless gas and has a broad flame.

The whole aim is to light the foot of the cigar evenly and gently, so the cigar, not in the mouth at this stage, must be rotated slowly just above and not in the flame; the cigar should not actually come into contact with the flame at any stage. Lighting a cigar properly is a little like the method used for toasting a marshmallow evenly over a campfire. The cigar should be rotated slowly until a glowing ring appears evenly all the way round the foot. Once lit, a gentle blow on the embers will complete the process and create a smooth, round burn.

Now the cigar can be smoked and enjoyed, although most smokers usually blow out the very first puff. Most cigar smokers also do not inhale the smoke into the lungs at all, except when smoking very small cigars. The smoke is instead swirled around the mouth and then exhaled, often through the nose and mouth, which enhances both the smell and taste of the cigar.

Personal preference to a cigar's taste is no different to that of food, wine and beer, and everyone's taste sensations react differently to each other. Although inevitably one person's pleasure can be another person's poison, there are some basic rules of thumb that connoisseurs use to differentiate an excellent cigar from a bad one that would benefit any cigar smoker in terms of maximising the enjoyment of smoking and forming more informed opinions about different cigars.

Art and Etiquette

All of the five senses, sight, touch, smell, taste and hearing, should be used for serious cigar appreciation. Touch and sight are the first two senses utilised before the cigar is even lit. Every cigar should be inspected and felt carefully first as its feel and appearance can tell an experienced smoker quite a lot, even about its taste. The wrapper is the first thing you see, and although its appearance will differ depending on where the leaf was grown, it should feel and look beautiful, unbroken, with a silky oiliness and be blemish free.

The slight oiliness in a wrapper leaf is a very good indication that the cigar has been stored correctly, i.e. humidified well. This also means that the cigar will burn cool, which produces a tastier smoke. If the cigar tobacco burns too hot it overheats, carbonises and the overall flavours are reduced.

The cigar wrapper does not totally dictate the overall flavour but does have some influence depending on its variety, origin and how it was processed. In general terms, a cigar with a darker wrapper tends to be sweeter than those with lighter wrappers, which give a drier taste to the overall smoke.

Listening to a cigar by rolling it between fingers before lighting is also very important. This shows the moisture content or lack of it in the cigar, of both wrapper and filler. A bad sign of a dry cigar can therefore be spotted easily if any crackling or rustling of leaves is heard. Ideally a cigar should be quite firm to the touch but compress a little when squeezed.

The tongue and, to a certain extent, the roof of the mouth is where taste messages are sensed and sent to the brain. There are four basic taste sensations: salty, bitter, sweet and sour, and different parts of the tongue register each separate element. Every kind of flavour and taste, even complex ones, comes from a combination of these four basic taste sensors.

The way connoisseurs describe the flavours and aromas of cigars is becoming similar to the often food-flavour descriptions and terms used by professional wine tasters. Traditionally, however, words such as balanced, rich, full-

Art and Etiquette

bodied, acidic, salty, sweet, sour, bitter, smooth and heavy are used to describe a cigar's flavour and overall character.

Aroma is also integral to a cigar's overall character and taste. Without our sense of smell working efficiently, our sense of taste is impaired severely; the two go hand in hand. Cigar makers have to balance both taste and aroma when creating blends of tobacco that work together in harmony. Often combining tobaccos that come from several different growing regions, variety grades and harvests creates the best blends. Balance and consistency are the two most difficult aspects the cigar-maker has to deal with. Tobacco is after all a natural product and is affected, as with most agricultural crops, by climate, soil, plant variety, production method and storage. No two tobacco leaves are the same, so no two cigars can ever be identical year after year, and every variety and brand of cigar produces a different taste.

The two final factors that have a serious influence on a cigar's overall taste are ageing and construction. Cigars that have been aged properly develop a rich, round and smooth character that would otherwise be lacking.

If the cigar has been constructed badly at the roller's table and somehow slipped through the net, which does unfortunately happen as with any handmade product, a cigar with even the finest blend of tobacco will be less enjoyable than a perfectly constructed one even made with an average tobacco blend. A bad construction affects the entire smoking experience: if a cigar is under filled (known as a loose draw) the smoking temperature will be too high as it burns too quickly and the taste will therefore be ruined; too tight a draw (i.e. too much filler tobacco) and less smoke is drawn through the cigar resulting in ultimately less taste. Cigars with a tight draw also have the tendency to go out more often and more easily. Ideally a fine cigar should burn consistently and be smoked without relighting if possible as relighting can cause harshness in taste.

Appreciating fine cigars is very much like appreciating fine food and wine. Cigars can generate different flavours throughout a smoke as the different tobaccos blended burn. This also means that each puff can taste different resulting

Art and Etiquette

in changing aftertastes as well. The presence of food or drink can also create wonderful taste variations for the smoker.

Smoking fine cigars is one of life's pleasures and should be relaxing, elegant and certainly not rushed. There are some basic techniques and faux pas, however, which every cigar smoker should have knowledge of in order to gain maximum enjoyment and minimum embarrassment or stress out of doing it.

Once the cigar is initially lit and that first puff has been expelled quickly, the rest of the cigar can be smoked at a leisurely pace allowing time for all the tastes and aromas to arouse the senses. Allowing the smoke to swirl round the mouth, without actually inhaling, will maximise the cigar's flavours. Time should also be taken between puffs. It is absolutely fine to rest the cigar in an ashtray from time to time, and a well-made cigar should stay lit as long as it is not left there for more than a minute or so at a time without being smoked.

A habit not to be encouraged is that of chewing the cigar or even holding it in the teeth whilst doing something else with the hands. Firstly, this probably means that relaxation and leisurely smoking is not on the agenda, but more importantly the end of the cigar becomes overly wet and the opening from which to draw the smoke can collapse in a mushy mess, which is both unpleasant and unsightly.

A cigar should be held correctly at all times and it should feel comfortable and controlled. A popular technique amongst connoisseurs is to hold the cigar between the thumb and the index and/or middle finger. The cigar must not be squeezed too tightly as this may seriously damage its structure or prevent the smoke from passing through it easily; holding it firmly yet gently is the key.

Apart from in the comfort of the home, private social gatherings are now one of the few occasions when a cigar may be enjoyed inside, with a drink, and in the company of good friends. If fortunate enough to have a host who allows or even enjoys cigar smoking, it is imperative that this is respected. It is not uncommon for regular smokers to

Art and Etiquette

partake in contests such as 'who can grow the longest ash on the end of the cigar'. This may be absolutely fine in some circumstances, but dropping large amounts of cigar ash on furniture or carpet is most definitely a serious breach of etiquette. Whilst some smokers may argue that cigar ash is actually good for carpet, the host will probably not agree, so always use an ashtray and flick the ash off before it drops off.

Cigar-smoking etiquette should be fairly obvious and using common sense and courtesy at all times should go without saying. There are, however, some basic dos and don'ts that may help the novice or uninitiated cigar smoker avoid embarrassing situations, especially if in the company of regular and experienced smokers:

Always exhale cigar smoke away from other people's faces, regardless of whether they are smokers or non-smokers.

Offer a lighter by all means, but never help someone light a cigar unless expressly requested to do so. Cigar lighting is a very personal thing and part of most smokers' overall enjoyment of a good cigar; the same rules apply to cutting.

Always wait to be offered a cigar from someone's collection or humidor. Even though some friends would not mind the fridge being opened or wine being poured without invitation, taking a cigar without asking is a serious faux pas, however close the friends are.

Never take more than one cigar when offered a selection.

Never grind a cigar out in an ashtray as this releases unnecessary and unpleasant odours. Leave it sitting in an ashtray for a few minutes and it will extinguish itself.

Art and Etiquette

Drinking With Cigars

Premium hand-rolled cigars can be exquisite smoked on their own, but can be equally enjoyable and arguably enhanced if accompanied by a spirit or glass of wine. Choice of drink is naturally influenced by personal preference and social occasion, but spirits such as Cognac, whisky and rum, and port or some wines are particularly popular and complimentary as an accompaniment with a fine cigar.

Cognac is traditionally the most popular spirit chosen to drink with a fine cigar as the oak-barrel aging and clean flavours keeps the palate on its toes ready to receive the complimentary smooth and sometimes spicy flavours of a cigar.

Whisky, particularly single-malt Scotch, and aged rums all have depth and complexity of flavours that stand up well and can compliment a cigar. Single malts made from smoked peat marry especially well. The slightly sweet yet subtle burnt molasses character of aged rum can actually make a cigar taste smoother that it would without.

Port is another traditional choice. The strength and sweetness of a vintage port is a particularly good match with a full-bodied cigar. Even non-vintage and younger ports have the woody characteristics and high tannin levels that make them perfect with a spicy cigar.

Wine is perhaps not such an obvious or traditional choice of drink. There are, however, particular regions and grape varieties from which the wine produced certainly compliments a smoke. Cabernet Sauvignon red wines from both California and Bordeaux are reliable suitors, as are the Rhône Valley wines made from Syrah, Grenache and Mourvèdre grape varieties.

Buying and Storing Cigars

◆

Regardless of whether a novice or experienced cigar smoker is looking to buy one cigar for a special occasion or cases to add to a collection, the most important person to seek and know is a good tobacconist. Not only will a good tobacconist get to know the personal preferences of a regular customer over time, they can help and advise the novice smoker and introduce a variety of different cigars to them that will suit their preferred taste.

A good tobacconist will also look after and store all the cigars at the correct humidity and temperature so that there can be no doubt as to the condition of any cigar in the shop. They will also be able to demonstrate that they are totally up-to-date with the cigar industry and will know what is available and what is not, and what kind of tobacco is being used to make the cigars all over the world.

A legendary story reputedly told by the late Zino Davidoff highlights the epitome of loyalty and service from a tobacconist: when the Dunhill shop in London was bombed in the World War II Blitz, it is said that the shop manager's first priority was to inform one of his best clients, Prime Minister Winston Churchill, that his favourite cigars had not been destroyed and were safe.

Buying and Storing Cigars

Local, reliable and knowledgeable tobacconists are not, however, that easy to find and many different shops may stock premium, hand-rolled cigars, but that doesn't necessarily mean they should be bought from them. There are some easy warning signs that should be looked for if buying from a new or unfamiliar supplier.

First be aware of the storage conditions of the cigars when asking to see them. If the tobacconist has a purpose-built walk-in humidor that feels moist and fairly chilly, then the likelihood is that the cigars will have been looked after with great care. If, however, there is some doubt, or the cigars are handed over from a dusty display cabinet or from the back room hidden from view, it is perfectly acceptable to ask to feel a cigar. If the cigar is intact, supple, and its wrapper oils are evident, then it will most likely be in perfectly good condition to smoke. It would certainly be most sensible to walk away if a request to feel a cigar was not granted.

Whilst asking to feel a cigar is perfectly acceptable behaviour, this has to be done in a very careful manner. All that is being established is that the cigar is not dry, old and hasn't been stored carelessly. This only requires a gentle squeeze to ascertain. Pressing it too hard can break the wrapper and totally ruin a perfectly good cigar, not to mention irritating the tobacconist immensely. Finally, also unacceptable is the act of putting the open foot of a cigar to the nose and smelling it (unless it has been bought and is being enjoyed prior to lighting). This has in the past been fairly common practice but is now seen as particularly unhygienic, added to the fact that, except for the professional connoisseur, the majority of even experienced cigar smokers wouldn't have a clue what they were actually smelling for.

Fine cigars are a natural product and therefore susceptible and sensitive to the environment in the same way that wine, beer, fresh food produce or any other natural, organic products are. This means that care has to be taken after buying cigars to keep them in perfect condition before smoking.

Buying and Storing Cigars

Cigars should always be stored in a humidor, which is a storage container that keeps the environment at a stable temperature and humidity level, very similar to the conditions in which the tobacco was grown. If stored properly they can in fact be kept in perfect condition for years at a time. It only takes a few hours for a cigar to dry out and be ruined if it is left out in a normal heated or air-conditioned room. A dry cigar will therefore burn faster and hotter and the maximum enjoyment of the flavour will be affected. Equally, if a cigar is allowed to become too damp, it will not burn evenly and can take on an unpleasant acidic quality when smoked. Well-humidified cigars burn evenly and at the correct temperature.

The ideal humidity range should be between seventy and seventy-two percent with an internal temperature of about twenty or twenty-one degrees Celsius. Humidors are available in many different sizes and serious fine cigar smokers may have a large one at home and a separate smaller portable one that holds one or two day's supply. Unfortunately good humidors are fairly expensive, and it is pointless buying one that does not do the job properly. The investment in fine cigars, however, requires an investment in the right equipment, very much like a wine connoisseur or collector has to do in order to keep a wine cellar in perfect condition to maximise the investment outlay.

For occasional fine cigar smokers and those who buy them to smoke straight away, a cigar can be kept in good condition for a day or so by putting it in a sealed plastic bag with a drop of water or piece of damp kitchen towel inside. If cigars do dry out then it is a sad fact but, unless handled by someone with a great deal of patience and experience, the cigar has to be thrown away and lessons learnt as to why it dried out in the first place. A skilled smoker with a very good humidor can in some cases very slowly, over weeks, recondition a dried-out cigar but this is very difficult to get right. There are also a few myths about how to restore a dry cigar that should also be thrown out with it: putting them in a steaming shower room will not work, nor will trying to recondition them by steaming on a rack in a dishwasher, or any other type of steam emitting appliance for that matter.

Cigars and Society

◆

Smoking cigars or cigarettes in public places has become a contentious issue all over the developed world as more and more anti-smoking campaigns support government smoking-ban legislations. Cigar smoke in particular is viewed very dimly by the non-smoking population mainly due to the fact that the smoke is thicker, takes longer to disperse, and is more aromatic than the smoke from a cigarette. Ironically, most smokers, even those who normally only smoke cigarettes, actually prefer and even enjoy the smell of a fine cigar.

The popularity and regulations regarding cigar smoking varies from country to country and even region to region. The United States are by far the top cigar smokers, followed by Germany and the United Kingdom. Approximately seventy-five percent of the world's cigar sales come from Western Europe and the United States.

Compared with only a decade ago, it is now much more difficult to go out and enjoy a cigar in a public place. Some thoughtful restaurants and bars, in response to their own downturn in sales due to smoking bans, do now provide well-lit, ventilated and heated smoking areas outside of the building, but the cigar smoker still has to decamp from the dining table to end a good meal with a fine cigar. The only other option is to eat outside in the first place, but even then many establishments have restrictions on smoking at tables that are in the close proximity of other diners.

Smoking cigars has historically been viewed as an activity suitable for men in society and the social perception

Cigars and Society

that smoking cigars is 'unladylike', unsanitary and far too masculine has been prevalent for centuries. In Paris in 1845, visiting Russian nobleman Wilhelm de Lenz would leave the room rather than be in the presence of a woman smoking a cigar. The French General Galliffet reputedly invited women, who dared light a cigar in his presence, to join him in the men's room.

There have, of course, always been female social rebels in the past, but even they usually confined their cigar-smoking habits to the privacy of their own homes. Strangely, even the decades of hedonism and women's emancipation of the 1960's and 1970's didn't address the gender-biased cigar-smoking taboo. By the 1980's it was still more likely that a woman would be successfully running a company that sold cigars rather than actually smoking them herself.

In Europe in particular attitudes began to shift to a certain extent during the 1990's and wealthy, well-dressed women began to choose cigars, albeit small ones, over cigarettes. Since then this has become much more socially acceptable and almost part of a wealthy, successful and powerful woman's list of accessories to accompany the designer shoes, handbag and sunglasses. The sight of a woman smoking a cigar is, however, generally still a controversial one that grabs attention, and most men either love it or despise it.

In more recent years the notion that women who smoke cigars are sexier and somehow more naughty or rebellious than their non-or cigarette-smoking counterparts has also become a modern-day phenomenon. The 1996 Hollywood film *The First Wives Club* very much played on this, as revenge-seeking wives played by Bette Midler, Goldie Hawn, and Diane Keaton, brandished their cigars with pride.

Some women smoke cigars purely for the affect that it has on the opposite sex, but there is now a growing number throughout the world who choose cigars over cigarettes purely for pleasure and because that really is their preferred choice.

Cigars and Society

At last, in the twenty-first century, women can do exactly as they want and are no longer forced to bow to the social taboos of the not-so-distant past. That does not necessarily mean that the majority of men's attitudes on the subject have shifted dramatically. Many men still don't like the fact that women can race sports cars, fly fast jets, fight for their country and head-up multi-million pound businesses, that thankfully no longer stops them doing it either.

The health implications of cigar smoking are, unfortunately, not as negligible as cigar smokers often like to think. There has been for many years a misconception that due to the fact that the cigar smoke is not inhaled into the lungs the health risk associated is far less than that of a cigarette smoker. To a certain extent this is true, but any exposure to tobacco-dominant products can cause medical problems even if the risks are not as great for cigars.

Risk does depend on dosage and heavy smokers will always be more at risk than the occasional smoker. Smokers of small cigars can also be more susceptible to linked diseases as there is a tendency to inhale the smoke in the same way a cigarette smoker would. It has now been medically proven that cigar smokers are exposed to many of the same health risks as cigarette smokers. Cigar smoking increases the risk of mouth, throat and oesophagus cancers and, if not inhaled, to a lesser but still some degree cancer of the lung and larynx. The risk of lung, and heart diseases such as chronic obstructive pulmonary disease is increased with all smoking.

Famous Cigar Smokers

The image of fine cigar smoking is often synonymous with the perception and symbolism of pure masculinity and power. Not only have some of the world's most iconic figures smoked fine cigars, but also famous images of them often feature a cigar. The tales and legends of men's smoking-room banter from the past is both intriguing and fascinating. Some of the most famous and influential people in the world have all had one thing in common, the love of a good cigar.

Cigars and Society

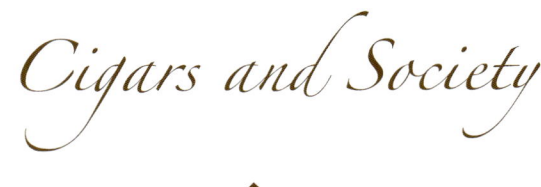

Sir Winston Churchill

Prime minister of the United Kingdom during the years of World War II and widely recognised as one of the greatest wartime leaders, Churchill (right) was renowned for his love of fine food, drink and cigars. He favoured Cuban cigars in particular, his favourite being the Romeo y Julieta. He smoked around ten cigars a day and the imposing 'Churchill' cigar was named after him in his honour. It is reputed that he even had a mask made specifically to allow him to enjoy his cigars when flying in a non-pressurised cabin at high altitude.

King Edward VII

Due to the fact that Edward VII's mother, Queen Victoria despised everything about smoking and would not tolerate it under her rule, he famously said following her death in 1901: 'Gentlemen, you may proceed to smoke.' His love of cigar smoking was well established by that time, however, and in 1866 he left his London gentlemen's club after they imposed a non-smoking policy.

Fidel Castro

Fidel Castro ruled Cuba with an iron fist for forty years and his reputation as a cigar lover is as well known as his reputation as Cuba's leader. His favourite cigar was the Cohiba Corona, but he gave up smoking them in 1985 as an example to his people following the medical warnings released at the time about the dangers of smoking. His love of cigars never waned, and although he never smoked them again, he admitted dreaming about them instead.

Cigars and Society

John F. Kennedy

Thirty-fifth President of the United States and a lover of Cuban cigars. Before signing the Cuban trade embargo, however, President John F. Kennedy and his aide Pierre Salinger managed to secure a stockpile of twelve hundred of his favourite Cuban cigars, the Petit Upmann.

Napoleon III of France

Louis-Napoleon Bonaparte was the President of the French Second Republic and as Napoleon III, the ruler of the Second French Empire from 1852 to 1870. In response to pressure to enforce a smoking ban, Napoleon III said, 'I will certainly forbid it at once, as soon as you can name a virtue that brings in as much revenue.'

Sigmund Freud

Even though Sigmund Freud (right) was renowned for seeing phallic symbols in everything, the father of psycho-analysis had to admit that 'sometimes a cigar is just a cigar'. Freud smoked cigars from the age of twenty-four and smoked about twenty a day; he was rarely seen without one in his hand. He viewed cigar smoking as one of life's greatest pleasures and claimed that he could not do the work he did without his cigars. He smoked throughout his lifetime and his favourite cigars included Don Pedros, Reina Cubanas and Dutch Liliputanos.

Mark Twain

Author of *Huckleberry Finn* and *The Adventures of Tom Sawyer*, Mark Twain smoked between twenty and forty cigars a day. He famously once declared that 'if smoking isn't allowed in heaven, I shall not go'. His penchant for cigars didn't necessarily mean that they were fine cigars, and Twain smoked anything except Havanas. He was well known amongst his friends for his collection of not-so-prestigious cigars.

Cigars and Society

Rudyard Kipling

English Nobel Prize winning author and poet, and lover of fine cigars. Rudyard Kipling became famous amongst cigar smokers and offended many women by writing the following line in his poem *The Betrothed*: 'And a woman is only a woman, but a good cigar is a smoke.'

Lord Byron

The famous English poet was so fond of smoking fine cigars that he wrote an ode to them called *Sublime Tobacco*.

Other famous female cigar smokers from the past include Greta Garbo, Annie Oakley, Mae West, Marlene Dietrich, and Bette Davis.

Hollywood actors and actresses are often known for their cigar smoking and therefore often captured on camera with a cigar in hand. Famous modern cigar-smoking Hollywood women include Madonna, Whoopi Goldberg, Demi Moore, Drew Barrymore, Lauren Hutton, Jodie Foster and Nicole Kidman to name a few.

The current generation of male cigar-smoking Hollywood stars includes Bruce Willis, Sylvester Stallone, Jack Nicholson, Danny DeVito, Arnold Schwarzenegger and Jim Belushi, to name a few.

GIFT BOOKS

You *Can* Judge a Book by its Cover!

Exclusively Distributed in North America by

pavilion gift
C O M P A N Y ®

www.tootsgiftbooks.com